— BEADED JEWELRY —
WIREWORK
TECHNIQUES

Skills, Tools, and Materials for
Making Handcrafted Jewelry

Carson Eddy, Rachael Evans, and Kate Feld

Storey Publishing

The mission of Storey Publishing is to serve our customers by publishing practical information that encourages personal independence in harmony with the environment.

Edited by Lisa H. Hiley and Nancy D. Wood
Series and cover design by Alethea Morrison
Art direction by Jeff Stiefel
Text production by Theresa Wiscovitch
Indexed by Christine R. Lindemer, Boston Road Communications

Cover illustration by © Caitlin Keegan
Interior Illustrations by © Kate Feld

Storey Publishing
210 MASS MoCA Way
North Adams, MA 01247
www.storey.com

Printed in the United States by McNaughton & Gunn, Inc.
10 9 8 7 6 5 4 3 2 1

LIBRARY OF CONGRESS CATALOGING-IN-PUBLICATION DATA

Eddy, Carson.
  Beaded jewelry. Wirework techniques : skills, tools, and materials for making hand crafted jewelry / Carson Eddy, Rachael Evans, and Kate Feld.
       pages cm. — (A Storey basics title)
  Includes index.
  ISBN 978-1-61212-484-1 (pbk. : alk. paper) — ISBN 978-1-61212-485-8 (ebook) 1. Beadwork. 2. Jewelry making. 3. Wire craft I. Evans, Rachael, 1980- II. Feld, Kate, 1982- III. Storey Publishing. IV. Title. V. Title: Wirework techniques.
TT860.E287 2014
745.594'2—dc23
                                        2014028194

CONTENTS

We dedicate this book to our moms,
who taught each of us a love of
learning and a passion for creativity.

INTRODUCTION

Metal is the foundation material for making wire, chain, and jewelry-making findings. Humans have been using metals in some way or another since the beginning of civilization. As long ago as 6000 BCE, the Egyptians, followed by the Greeks and Romans, were making decorative objects and jewelry from gold. A basic understanding of metallurgy, the science of working and shaping metal, is useful for anyone interested in creating jewelry with these materials.

Metals are either elements or alloys. Elements are the basic building blocks of chemistry; metal elements are unique because they reflect light, are malleable, can be fused, and conduct heat and electricity. Naturally occurring metal elements in their pure form are generally not very useful because they are too soft, too hard, or too brittle. To be useful for jewelry making, metal elements with different qualities are combined to make more useful metal alloys.

Wire, chain, and jewelry-making findings come in a wide range of metals, gauges, and styles. A little assistance when shopping for wire and metal products can go a long way. Local bead shops, staffed by knowledgeable jewelry makers, are usually an excellent resource. Some alloys may contain metals that are known to cause allergies or to be carcinogenic, so shopping in person is always the best way to ensure that you get what you expect!

We hope you will find this book useful and keep it close at hand for many years to come.

Carson, Rachael, and Kate

A Word about Lead

Lead is worth mentioning in any discussion about jewelry metals. Traditionally, lead has been used as an ingredient in a number of alloys, as it makes an alloy more malleable and lowers its melting temperature. Today lead is known to contribute to a variety of health problems. State and local governments have begun to regulate the amount of lead permitted in products, especially jewelry products that may be handled by children. To date, California is the only state that also regulates lead content in adult jewelry.

CHAPTER ONE

WIRE BASICS

Wire is metal that has been stretched into long, thin, flexible filaments. It is an incredibly versatile material with a multitude of applications. Wire can be used to make structures, to link elements together, and to add decorative interest. Many types of wire are available in a full range of metals, sizes, shapes, and finishes, perfect for all kinds of jewelry-making projects.

WIRE TYPES

WHEN PEOPLE BEGIN MAKING wire-based jewelry and findings, the question of wire type always arises. The kind of project being made and personal preference are generally the deciding factors. There are two types of wire used in jewelry making: *flexible beading wire*, which is used exclusively for stringing beads, and *hard wire*, which is used for wireworking. Each type of wire comes in a variety of diameters or gauges and colors; hard wire also comes in a variety of shapes.

Flexible Beading Wire

Flexible beading wire is one of the most popular materials used for stringing beaded jewelry. This strong but flexible, nylon-coated, stainless steel wire is secured to a clasp with crimp beads. Two popular brands of flexible beading wire are SoftFlex and Beadalon. These brands offer the highest-quality choices in a variety of diameters, flexibilities, and colors. In addition to the standard silver, gold, and metal colors, flexible beading wire comes in a range of seasonal colors, as well as black and white.

When selecting a flexible beading wire for a stringing project, it is best to select the thickest one that will comfortably fit through the beads being used. Different diameters of flexible beading wire are recommended for different sizes and weights of beads.

Very fine diameter (.010 to .013 inch) is best used with tiny, lightweight beads, gemstones, or pearls with very small drill holes. This diameter wire drapes nicely as long as the beads being used are light enough.

Fine diameter (.014 to .015 inch) is recommended for general-purpose stringing projects using light- to medium-weight beads. Seed beads, crystals, and Czech glass beads string and drape nicely on this diameter wire. Avoid using heavy beads with this diameter beading wire, as excess weight can pull the wire out of the crimps and lead to loss.

Medium diameter (.018 to .019 inch) is recommended for medium-weight beads, large glass beads, or stone beads, as well as for projects that need extra durability. This diameter of beading wire is very popular for bracelet and necklace projects that are worn frequently or that are made with larger or heavier beads.

Heavy diameter (.024 inch) is suggested for projects that get a lot of use, such as bracelets, lanyards, and eyeglass holders. This diameter wire works well with very large or heavy beads, including lampwork beads, African trade beads, and beads made from bone and stone. It is also appropriate for beads with large holes or holes that may be rough or abrasive.

Another variable to consider when selecting flexible beading wire is the number of strands of stainless steel from which a particular beading wire is made. The more strands this type of wire is made from, the sturdier and more flexible it will be. Beadalon produces a good-quality wire made with only seven strands of stainless steel. This wire is the least flexible option but is ideal for craft projects or children's jewelry.

Both SoftFlex and Beadalon produce better-quality beading wires made with 19 or 21 strands of stainless steel. These beading wires are stronger and more flexible than 7-strand beading wire. Both brands of 19- and 21-strand beading wire are popular and cost effective for general purpose bead stringing, and they drape nicely when used with appropriately sized beads. The best-quality beading wires that SoftFlex and Beadalon produce are made with 49 strands of stainless steel. These beading wires are by far the strongest and most flexible, and withstand the most wear. They are highly recommended for working with valuable beads.

Hard Wire

Hard wire is the type of wire used for making wire-based jewelry and findings. It is most commonly used for wire wrapping, creating linked chain, and making wire-based findings. Hard wire is an amazing material to work with because it is fluid yet sturdy, soft yet hard, and creates a lovely finished product.

There are three types of hard wire used in wireworking: precious metal wire, base metal wire, and memory wire. It is important to consider the attributes of each type of hard wire when selecting one to work with. Things to consider include material (metal type), temper (hardness), diameter (gauge), and shape. The following pages explore these attributes. For a descriptive list of metal types, see the appendix (page 78).

PRECIOUS METAL WIRES

Precious metal wires produce both beautiful and valuable pieces of jewelry. These wires may be the most expensive, but they produce the best results and should always be used when making heirloom or keepsake jewelry. Karat gold and fine or sterling silver are the most popular precious metal wires for making wire jewelry and components. Each type of precious metal wire comes in a range of tempers, gauges, and shapes.

- **Karat gold wire** is the most expensive wire available and is often hard to source. The term *karat* refers to the percentage of pure gold found in various gold alloys and is designated with a "K" after the percentage. The color and value of gold wire depends on its gold content. Gold wire is most often available in 24K, 18K, and 14K gold. For a comparison of karat weight for a variety of gold alloys, see the appendix (page 79).

- **Gold-filled wire**, also known as **rolled gold wire**, is made by permanently bonding a 14- or 18-karat gold layer to a solid brass or copper core and then drawing it through a series of draw plates to the desired gauge. Gold-filled wire is popular because it is more affordable than karat gold wire and is essentially the same color because of the gold content. Since gold-filled wire is made with a lot more gold than gold-plated wire, it tends to be more flexible and certainly more durable. For a product to be labeled as gold-filled, it must contain a minimum of $\frac{1}{20}$ pure gold by overall weight.

- **Rose gold wire** is made from an alloy of gold, copper, and, depending on the color, a small percentage of fine silver. The addition of copper to the alloy gives rose gold its warm, rosy tone. The greater the copper content the redder the coloration of the alloy. Typical 18-karat rose gold wire is made of 75 percent gold, 22.25 percent copper, and 2.75 percent fine silver.

- **White gold wire** is made from an alloy of gold and silver metal, usually palladium. A common 18-karat white gold is made from an alloy of 75 percent gold and 25 percent palladium. The addition of palladium makes for a softer, more pliable metal alloy, ideal for wire and findings. For sturdier or heavier gauge items like rings and pins, nickel is added to the alloy in place of the palladium. If you suffer from a nickel allergy, it is always good to ask about the nickel content of white gold wire or findings before purchasing them.

- **Fine silver wire** is not an alloy like sterling silver. It is 99.9 percent pure silver with the balance being made up of trace impurities. Fine silver is generally too soft for making functional objects, but it makes wonderfully fluid wire that can easily be work-hardened. Because fine silver does not contain any copper, it will not oxidize or blacken when heated. This quality makes fine silver ideal for fusing and annealing if it is work-hardened too much.

- **Sterling silver wire** is made from an alloy of 92.5 percent pure silver and 7.5 percent copper. It is one of the most popular wires for wire wrapping, making linked chain, and for making wire-based findings. Due to its popularity, an abundance of ready-made clasps and earring findings is available to complement any wire project. Sterling silver is exceptionally easy to work with, is consistent in color, and comes in a wide range of gauges, tempers, and shapes.

- **Argentium** wire is made from a modern sterling silver alloy that contains 93.5 percent pure silver and 6.5 percent copper and germanium. Since the alloy contains 93.5 percent pure silver, it meets the legal standard to be marked as sterling silver. Argentium is bright white in color and looks more like fine silver than traditional sterling. The tiny percentage of germanium gives this alloy an increased natural tarnish resistance.

- **Silver-filled wire** has a solid copper or brass alloy core bonded with a layer of sterling silver. Silver-filled wire is more durable than silver-plated wire because the bonded layer of sterling silver is much thicker. The bonded layer does not wear off with use as the layer of silver on silver-plated wire tends to. Silver-filled wire is a great-looking and cost-effective alternative to sterling silver wire.

BASE METAL WIRES

Base metal wires are most often plated, colored, or coated, although raw copper and raw brass wires are also available. These wires are cost-effective alternatives to precious metal wires.

"Plated" is a term that means different things to different people. Plated wire generally refers to a base metal wire that has been electroplated with another metal. Craft wire is often mistakenly referred to as plated wire. Craft wire is actually a base metal or aluminum wire that has been coated, colored, or finished, rather than electroplated.

Base metal wires are a versatile option for jewelry and craft projects since they come in a nice range of qualities, colors, and finishes. There are three main types of base metal wire: German-style plated wire, raw wire, and craft wire.

Tech Tip

Base metal wires are practical for practicing wirework. One rule of thumb is to practice twice using base metal wire before making a final piece in precious metal wire.

GERMAN WIRE

German wire is the best-quality plated base metal wire available. German beading wires have an antitarnish coating and are the perfect temper for most wire-wrapping projects. The highest-quality German beading wires are made in Germany. Lower-quality German-style beading wires are made in the United States. Both German and German-style wires come in a range of tempers, gauges, and fancy shapes.

- **Copper** and **brass German wires** have a copper or brass-alloy core that is finished with an antitarnish coating. These wires are not electroplated or colored.

- **Silver** and **gold German wires** are made with a copper core that is electroplated with precious metal and finished with an antitarnish coating. Gold German wire is plated with 14-karat gold, and silver German wire is plated with sterling silver. These wires provide the closest color match to their precious metal counterparts.

RAW WIRE

Raw wire is solid copper or brass-alloy wire that is not plated or coated with an antitarnish finish. Because the raw metal wire is uncoated, it tends to oxidize and darken very quickly.

- **Raw copper wire** is a very malleable wire that is perfect for beginners. It is easy to work with, great to practice on, and very cost-effective. Freshly polished raw copper has a warm, red-brown luster. As copper wire ages and oxidizes, it takes on a soft green patina.

- **Raw brass wire** is made from an alloy of copper and zinc that is similar in color to gold, especially after being freshly polished. Brass wire is less expensive than gold wire and easy to work with. It is a versatile wire that is good to practice with but will darken as it oxidizes.

CRAFT WIRES

Craft wires are the least expensive wires available and are produced by several manufacturers. Each brand varies in flexibility, metal content, and coating process. The proprietary coloring processes of these wires vary by manufacturer. Each brand of craft wire offers a nice range of both natural and seasonal colors in a range of gauges. Choosing a craft wire to work with is primarily a matter of personal preference.

- **Artistic Wire** is a popular brand of permanently colored copper wire. The proprietary enamel-coating process resists tarnishing, peeling, and chipping. Artistic Wire is flexible and easy to work with, making it a wonderful choice for children's jewelry and craft projects. It comes in 13 gauges and in silver, brass, and copper, as well as a wide range of seasonal colors.
- **Craft Wire**, manufactured in the United States by BeadSmith, is available in a nice range of colors to coordinate with just about every metal hue. This brand of craft wire is stiffer than others but is similar in flexibility to half-hard wire (see page 16). Craft Wire is very bright and shiny, and the tarnish-resistant coating helps to maintain the bright coloration over time.

- **Parawire** is made with a 99 percent copper core, and the company's exclusive coloring process produces the brightest colors of craft wire available. After being colored, the wires are coated with nylon for a durable finish. Parawire is softer than Craft Wire but harder than Artistic Wire.
- **SoftFlex craft wire** is permanently colored copper wire that is resistant to scratching, peeling, and marring. This brand of wire is 100 percent free of lead and nickel and is colored using a special enameling process. All SoftFlex craft wires, except for bare copper, are clear-coated to prevent tarnishing.

MEMORY WIRE

Memory wire is a unique steel wire material. It is made from tempered spring steel that always returns to its coil form when expanded and released. It is manufactured in ring, bracelet, and necklace diameters and is packaged in coils. Memory wire comes in several colors including silver, gold, and bronze; in round and flat wire shapes; and in round and oval coils.

WIRE ATTRIBUTES

WIRE HAS A VARIETY OF ATTRIBUTES that make it fun to work with. Each gauge (size) of wire is available in a range of shapes and tempers (hardness). Many types of wire have two particularly appealing attributes: they can be hardened by working with them, or softened by heating them.

Wire Gauge

Wire gauge refers to the diameter of round wire or the cross-sectional dimension of shaped wire. *Drawing* is the process of pulling a wire through one or more successively smaller dies on a draw plate to produce the gauge of a wire. As a wire is drawn, the temper (hardness) of the wire increases as well. Wire can be returned to a softer state by a heat process called *annealing.* This process allows wires to be manufactured in a wide range of gauges of varying tempers. Machine-made wire is annealed as it is drawn and coiled.

The gauge of a wire is defined by the number of times it is pulled through the draw plate or die. Unlike most systems of measurement, the higher the gauge number, the thinner the wire. A very fine 30-gauge wire requires far more passes through the draw plate than a heavy 16-gauge wire.

Several gauging systems are used around the world. The American Wire Gauge (AWG) system has been used in the United States since 1857. This conversion chart shows both the inch and millimeter diameters associated with common wire gauges used in jewelry making.

American Wire Gauge (AWG) Conversion Chart

GAUGE	INCHES	MILLIMETERS
16	0.051	1.29
18	0.04	1.02
20	0.036	0.812
22	0.025	0.723
24	0.02	0.573
26	0.016	0.405
28	0.013	0.321
30	0.01	0.255

Wire Shape

Wire is manufactured in several shapes, including round, half-round, and square. These shapes are produced when wire is drawn through a shaped die on a draw plate. Using different wire shapes can produce pretty jewelry and combining shapes can add interest to any wirework project.

Round wire is the most common shape for wire and can be used for almost any wirework project. Round wire is used for making most basic earring findings, including ear wires, head pins (defined on page 36), and eye pins (defined on page 35). It is also terrific for wrapping beads and for making jump rings and simple clasps.

Half-round wire is flat on one side and domed on the other. It is often used for wire wrapping, linking, and making rings and components. This low-profile style of wire is also used to bind bundles of square wire together in complex designs. The flat side of the half-round wire is placed against the side of a square wire so that the rounded side remains exposed in the finished design. This technique is called banding.

Square wire gives jewelry a completely different look and is frequently chosen for purely aesthetic reasons. The flat sides of square wire lie flush against one another in a way that round wire does not. The squared edges add unique interest to finished pieces of jewelry.

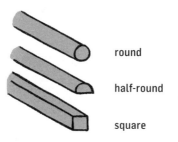

round

half-round

square

Twisted or **fancy wire** is primarily used to add textural interest to wireworking. It can be purchased ready-made or can be handmade by twisting round or square wires together with a wire-twisting tool.

Wire Temper

Wire temper describes the hardness or softness of a particular wire: its malleability, its ability to bend fluidly, and its tendency to hold a shape once bent. Wire temper can range from dead-soft (which bends with no resistance) to spring-hard (which is very resistant to bending). As wire or other types of metal are wrapped, hammered, or otherwise manipulated, they gradually become harder; this is called *work-hardening*. If wire becomes too hard, it can be softened by annealing. Using a small butane torch to anneal wire is a common metalworking technique.

It is important to purchase wire with the proper hardness for each individual project. Dead-soft or soft wire is ideal for soft bending or making coils or fluid shapes. Half-hard wire is the best choice for making sharp corners or for wrapping stones or beads. Full-hard wire is very stiff and challenging to work with but produces the sturdiest results.

Dead-soft and **soft (¼ hard) wires** are very malleable and can be work-hardened very easily. Be careful not to overwork dead-soft or soft wires as they can become brittle and excessively springy.

Half-hard wire is harder than soft wire but is still very manageable to work with. Half-hard wire, even in narrow gauges, feels sturdy and holds its shape after being worked.

Tech Tip

It can be helpful to use nylon-coated tools with heavier gauges of half-hard wire to prevent marring the surface of the wire. Both nylon-jaw tools and rubber tips that are used to coat the jaws of wireworking tools are available.

Full-hard wire is harder than half-hard wire and more difficult to manipulate. It tends to be very stiff and can be hard on the fingers. Full-hard wire is unforgiving if you make a mistake. Once hard wire is bent or shaped it can no longer be straightened.

Spring-hard wire has been tempered so that it will always spring back to its original coil form. Spring-hard wire is very difficult to work with and requires the use of specialized pliers and cutters. Memory wire is a good example of spring-hard wire.

SELECTING WIRE FOR A PROJECT

ALTHOUGH WIRE SELECTION IS largely a matter of personal preference, the choice should be guided by some basic rules of thumb. First and foremost, select a wire in the material that suits the components being used in a particular project. For example, if you are using precious metal findings and clasps for your project, use precious metal wire as well.

Choosing a Material

Precious metal wires such as fine silver, sterling silver, Argentium, silver-filled, karat gold, and gold-filled wire are suitable for almost any wirework project. For the most professional look, always coordinate the selected precious metal wire with findings and clasps of the same metal. Be certain to match metal color as closely as possible, especially when working with gold. Precious metal wire is always the best choice for making heirloom-quality jewelry.

Base metal wires are ideal for a wide variety of jewelry and craft projects. Base metal wires are available in silver-plated and gold-plated copper, raw and coated copper, brass, nickel silver, aluminum, and niobium. Base metal wires are also an excellent choice for practicing wirework techniques and for creating prototypes of jewelry that will eventually be made from precious metal wire.

Craft wires are relatively inexpensive, making them perfect for craft projects, children's jewelry, and other types of beginner jewelry. Craft wires are available in standard silver, brass, bronze, copper, and black colors. Each brand produces an assortment of brightly colored wires in a range of gauges.

Memory wire is a unique spring-hard wire that returns to its coiled shape when stretched and released. Due to this property, memory wire is ideal for stringing beads to make choker-style necklaces and multicoil bracelets and rings.

Choosing a Gauge

It is also important to consider the size of your bead holes. Always select the wire gauge that matches the smallest bead hole in your project.

14-gauge and **16-gauge wire** are ideal for hammering projects. These gauges are common choices for making heavier clasps, jump rings, eye pins for large-holed beads, frames, wire shapes, and bangles.

18-gauge and **20-gauge wire** are suitable for wireworking with larger beads. These gauges are a common choice for wire wrapping, and for making ear wires, head pins and eye pins, clasps, and jump rings. Most people use 20-gauge wire when making their own findings.

22-gauge and **24-gauge wire** are great for most jewelry projects and will fit through most beads, including gemstones and pearls. These gauges are commonly used for wire linking and wire wrapping.

26-gauge and **28-gauge wire** are used for delicate projects such as knitting or crocheting with wire, wrapping small gemstones, and linking gemstones and pearls. These gauges are also good for working with pearls that have very small holes.

30-gauge wire is essential for projects involving diamonds or semiprecious gemstone beads that have irregular or tiny holes. This gauge is also essential for making intricately woven wire designs.

Choosing a Temper

Selection of wire temper and wire shape should be based on project type and personal preference.

Dead-soft and **soft wire** are useful choices if the wire will be worked a lot (hammering, bending, and so on) before it is made into a finished piece. Dead-soft wire in a thin gauge behaves more like a fiber than a wire, making it very useful for knitting, crocheting, weaving, and coiling.

Half-hard wire is sturdy and will hold a shape. This popular wire temper is most commonly used for wire wrapping and for making ear wires, head pins, hoops, and clasps.

Full-hard wire is a less common choice because it is more difficult to work with. It is popular with experienced jewelry makers because it stands up to use longer than half-hard wire. It can be used to create clasps, ear wires, head pins, eye pins, and links or components.

Spring-hard wire, more commonly called memory wire, is used to make rings, bracelets, and necklaces that will always hold a circular or oval shape.

....

How Wire Is Sold

By weight: Karat gold wire is sold by the pennyweight, while gold-filled, sterling silver, and silver-filled wire are sold by the ounce.

By the roll: Craft wires are sold on spools of varying yardages, depending on the gauge and brand of the wire.

By the coil: German-style plated wire and raw wire are sold in coils of varying yardages, depending on the gauge of the wire. Memory wire, also available by the coil, is sold by numbers of revolutions.

By the foot: Precious metal and German-style plated wire are sold by prepackaged weight. Bead stores frequently sell these wires by the foot, and sometimes even by the inch.

....

CHAPTER TWO

CHAIN BASICS

Chain is a wonderfully varied material that is frequently used in jewelry making. Chain can be used as a design element in earrings, bracelets, and necklaces, as the foundation of a charm bracelet or pendant necklace, or for something as functional as a necklace extender.

CHAIN MATERIALS

CHAIN IS TYPICALLY MADE IN small factories that use complex machinery to draw, coil, link, and sometimes even solder metal wire into the various chain styles. Certain specialty chains, such as Thai Hill Tribe silver chain, are meticulously handcrafted by skilled artisans. Chain can also be made from materials such as wood, acrylic, and fiber.

The finest chains are made from 18- or 14-karat gold, gold-filled, fine silver, sterling silver, or platinum wire. The most popular and versatile chains are made from brass wire, which is available in both raw and plated metal. Raw brass and raw copper chains are commonly plated with a silver, antique silver, gold, antique copper, gunmetal, or antique brass finish. The plating process enhances the beauty of the chain, improves its durability, and reduces corrosion.

Other metals, including steel and aluminum, can also be used to make chain. Aluminum is particularly lightweight, and can be brightly colored by an electroplating process called *anodization*. For a descriptive list of metal types, see the appendix (page 78).

CHAIN TREATMENTS

CHAINS MADE FROM WIRE CAN BE altered in a number of ways to add variety and interest to the style or metal surface. The shape of links can be manipulated, textures can be added, and links can be soldered to make them more secure.

Soldered versus **unsoldered chain** is selected based on how the chain will be used in a particular project. Soldering closes and secures chain links so they will not stretch and gap, which can lead to breakage. Most precious metal chains are soldered. Other metals, such as copper, are not easily soldered. When working with unsoldered chain, the links should be substantial enough to handle normal wear without stretching. Individual links of unsoldered chain can be used as decorative components in jewelry projects like earrings.

Flattening is a process where wire links are flattened in a press to create more surface area that will reflect light. Flattened chain appears to be brighter and shinier.

Drawing chain, not to be confused with drawing wire, is a process of stretching round or oval links to elongate the shape of the links. Drawing chain changes its overall appearance and also makes it narrower.

Dapping can either curve a metal link or leave a single hammer strike mark on the link. Curved links add interest and hammer strikes add a surface texture that reflects light.

Hammering wire links creates a multifaceted surface. Different hammering techniques leave different marks on the metal surface. Any style of hammering adds reflectivity to the surface of wire chain links.

Texturing can be applied to the surface of metal or wire by imprinting textures ranging from simple lines to more complicated pattern imprints. Hammers with decorative heads are used to create a variety of textures.

Knurling is a common texture that gives chain links a cross-hatched surface texture that looks nice when oxidized.

Diamond cut patterns or angled facets are created on the surface of the metal using precision tools. This alteration creates the best light-catching facets possible.

CHAIN STYLES

CHAIN IS MANUFACTURED IN a nearly endless range of styles from simple cable chains to rhinestone cup chains. Style is defined by the shape of the links, the order of the linking, and in some cases, by the surface treatment of the links.

Cable chain is made by connecting round or oval links of wire together with each link lying at 90 degrees to the next. Cable chain is the simplest and most common chain used in jewelry making.

cable chain

Double cable link or **parallel cable chain** is made when two links are laid side by side in each link position.

- **Flat cable chain** is made from links that have been hammered flat.
- **Figure 8 chain** starts out as a basic cable chain, but then alternating links are twisted into a figure 8 (the shape of an infinity symbol).

Satellite chain is made from small round links with small beads added at even intervals that look like orbiting planets, adding interest and texture to the chain.

 satellite chain

Curb chain is made from oval links that have all been twisted, or "curbed," so the entire length of the chain lies flat against the body.

 curb chain

Double curb link or **parallel curb chain** is made when two curbed links are laid side by side in each link position.

Long-and-short chain is a chain style that is made from short, repeating patterns of links that are fairly uniform in width but differ in length.

long-and-short chain

- **Figaro chain** is a popular long-and-short variation made from a pattern of three short, curbed links followed by one long, curbed link that is the same length as the three short links.

Rollo chain and **belcher chain** are made from uniform round or oval links. These chain styles are heavier than cable chain and look like they have been assembled from strips of metal rather than from round wire.

rollo chain

- **Rollo chain** is made from uniform links of half-round wire.
- **Belcher chain** is made from uniform links of low-domed or flat wire.

Bar chain is made from bar-shaped links joined by small, oval ring connectors. The bars can be straight, curved, decorative, elongated, shaped, twisted, hollow, solid, or even a combination of these.

bar chain

Beaded chain or **rosary chain** is a series of wire-wrapped beads, pearls, or gemstones that are linked together.

beaded chain

Snake chain is a tubular chain made from an assembly of curved plates. Snake chains are highly flexible and have a solid appearance instead of open links.

snake chain

Ball chain is made from tiny spheres of metal rather than open links. These spheres or balls can be solid or hollow to reduce weight. They can be fixed at regular intervals along the length of the chain or fixed directly next to one another. This type of chain is also known as **bead chain** or **pelline chain**.

ball chain

Cup chain is made from a series of cup-style metal links that are set with glass or crystal rhinestones. The metal "cups" are generally square in shape with prongs at each corner to hold a round rhinestone in place. Cup chains come in a wide range of cup sizes, base metal types, and colors.

cup chain

CHAPTER THREE

FINDINGS BASICS

Most handcrafted wirework jewelry requires some type of finding to make it functional. Clasps keep necklaces and bracelets closed around the wearer's neck or wrist. Earring findings are used to suspend earring elements from the ears, while earring backs secure earrings to the ear. Other types and styles of findings improve functionality and add decorative interest.

CLASP FINDINGS

A MYRIAD OF STYLES OF clasps are available. Simple clasps include lobster claws, spring rings, and toggles. More specialized closures include tube and bar clasps, box clasps, and multistrand clasps. Selecting the best clasp for your project is partly a matter of taste, partly about design, and partly application.

Barrel clasps are two-piece clasps that screw together. This style of clasp comes in a range of shapes, sizes, and finishes.

barrel clasp

Box clasps are two-piece clasps that comprise a box and a small, pressure-fitted piece that snaps into the box. Some box clasps have tiny snap locks for extra security. This clasp is good for use with bracelets and necklaces. Box clasps come in lots of shapes, sizes, decorative designs, and metals from plated to precious.

box clasp

J-hooks are shaped pieces of metal that connect with soldered rings or jump rings on either end. This clasp is best used on necklaces and comes in simple and decorative styles. J-hooks come in a range of sizes and in metals from plated to precious.

J-hook

Lanyard clasps are thin, one-piece clasps shaped like a long drop with a flexible snap closure. This clasp is used mostly for identification lanyards or jewelry projects made of leather or hemp. Lanyard clasps are usually made from plated metals.

 lanyard clasp

Lobster claws are a very popular and secure clasp, frequently used with flexible beading wire and crimp beads. They can be used with just about any finding and stringing material to finish a jewelry project. This clasp is shaped like a lobster claw and comes in a variety of sizes, designs, and metals from plated to precious.

 lobster claw

Magnetic clasps are two-part clasps held together by strong magnets. This type of clasp is good for lightweight jewelry and for people who have trouble opening lobster claws or spring rings. Magnetic clasps come in a wide range of magnetic strengths, sizes, and designs.

 magnetic clasp

Pearl clasps are very traditional, oval-shaped clasps with filigree detail. This type of clasp has a unique hook and snap closure. Pearl clasps are traditionally made from precious metals but are now available in other metals as well.

pearl clasp

S-hooks are shaped pieces of metal that connect with soldered rings or jump rings on either end. This clasp is best used on necklaces, and it comes in simple and decorative styles. S-hooks come in a small range of sizes and in metals from plated to precious.

S-hook

Spring rings are shaped like a ring with a spring-loaded barrel. This clasp is frequently used with flexible beading wire and crimp beads. A spring ring can also be used with just about any finding and stringing material to finish a jewelry project. These clasps come in a variety of sizes and metals from plated to precious.

spring ring

Toggle clasps are made with two parts: a ring and a bar. The bar slides through the ring and then lies across it to close. This clasp is less secure than a lobster claw or spring ring but is often easier to use. Toggle clasps are made in a vast array of decorative designs and are often included as a design element in jewelry projects. These clasps come in a variety of sizes and metals from plated to precious.

toggle clasp

Tube and bar clasps typically have two parts that slide together and snap into place to form a tube with connection points on each side. These connection points are either bars that run the length of each side of the tube, or a series of two, three, five, or seven loops on each side of the tube. Some versions of these clasps are magnetic for added security. Tube and bar clasps are ideal for making multistrand necklaces or bracelets. They are available in plated and precious metals.

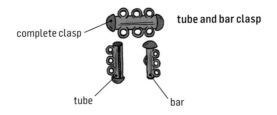

complete clasp

tube and bar clasp

tube

bar

EARRING FINDINGS

EARRING FINDINGS ARE MADE FOR both pierced and non-pierced ears in a wide range of styles, sizes, and materials. The most basic earring design is made from three components: an ear wire, a finding for attaching a decorative element to the ear wire, and a finding for securing the ear wire to the earlobe.

Shepherd's hook ear wires date back to Roman times. They are shaped like a shepherd's crook, consequently the name. This style of ear wire is similar to the fishhook/French wire but has a longer shaft.

shepherd's hook

Fishhook/French wire ear wires are curved at the top and have a hook-shaped shaft that passes through the pierced ear. This type of ear wire comes in a variety of styles.

fishhook/French wire
with ball

fishhook/French wire
with coil

fishhook/French
wire with ball
and coil

Add-a-bead is designed to add any bead and to finish with a loop.

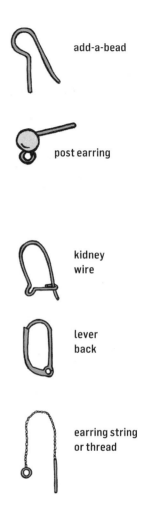

add-a-bead

Post earrings, sometimes called **stud with loop,** are a style of pierced earring that sits tight to the earlobe. A ball or decorative element is soldered to a stud that passes through the pierced ear. A loop from which the head pin hangs is then soldered to the front of the ball or decorative element. Post earrings come in a wide range of styles.

post earring

Kidney wires come in a variety of shapes and sizes. They are similar to the fishhook/French wire except they close for added security.

kidney wire

Lever backs are similar to fishhooks, but the hook actually snaps closed and has either a soldered or an unsoldered loop from which the head pin hangs.

lever back

Earring strings or **earring threads** are pieces of chain with a blunt pin that strings directly through the ear and a soldered loop from which the head pin hangs.

earring string or thread

Hoops come in a variety of sizes. Jewelry makers can wire-wrap beads around the hoop, string beads directly onto the hoop, or hang them from the hoop.

Clip-ons come in a variety of styles for nonpierced ears. The most common style is a ball with a loop from which the head pin, bead, or charm hangs. Other styles use a decorative element in place of the ball or provide a flat pad for gluing.

Screw back with loop is for non-pierced ears. The most common style is a ball with a loop from which the head pin, bead, or charm hangs. Other styles use a decorative element in place of the ball.

Eye pins are wire pins with a loop at the bottom for making earrings. They are also useful for making multisection earrings. Eye pins can be purchased ready-made or made by hand from a wide range of gauges and lengths.

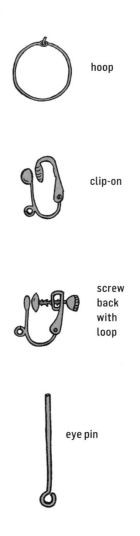

hoop

clip-on

screw
back
with
loop

eye pin

Head pins are wire pins with a flat or decorative bottom for making earrings. Basic head pins have a flat bottom simply to keep beads from falling off of the pin. Decorative head pins come in many different styles. Head pins can be purchased ready-made or made by hand from a wide range of gauges and lengths.

head pin

chandelier

Chandelier findings are decorative wire or metal elements that can be purchased or made in a multitude of shapes, gauges, and metals. Jewelry makers wire-wrap these components with beads, suspend beads from them, or combine them with other materials to make sensational earrings.

Earring Backs

Earring backs are an essential finding for securing earrings to the earlobe and to help prevent loss. They come in a variety of styles to both suit the wearer and match the earring.

Rubber earring backs slide onto the back of a fishhook and can be adjusted for tightness. The most common styles are made of either softer, white, spongy rubber or stiffer, clear plastic acrylic.

 rubber earring backs

Ear nuts are small, metal components used to keep a post earring secured to the earlobe. They come in several different sizes and in a variety of metals to match the metals of post earrings.

 ear nuts

Monster earring backs are dome-shaped ear nuts with a large, round, clear plastic disk attached to them. These backs are useful when wearing large or heavy post earrings. The plastic disk ensures that the earring fits snugly on the earlobe.

 monster earring backs

OTHER FINDINGS

THE ADDITION OF CAPS AND CONES is usually a decorative design choice. Caps are sometimes used to mask unsightly bead holes, and cones are often added to hide the ends of a multistrand project. Rings are used for practical reasons, most commonly to connect wire to findings, to add decorative elements to wire or chain, or as part of a closure.

Caps are decorative, half-sphere-shaped findings that fit over bead holes to disguise the opening or add to the design of the piece. They come in a complete range of designs, sizes, and metals from plated to precious.

caps

Cones are decorative, conical-shaped findings. They are used to conceal multiple strands of beads that attach to a single clasp. They come in a complete range of designs, sizes, and metals from plated to precious.

cones

Rings are made in a variety of metals so they will match other metals in a project. Each type of ring comes in a wide range of sizes and wire gauges, and each type of ring has a specialized use.

Jump rings are open, unsoldered rings that can be used to attach clasps, pendants, charms, and other components together or to a chain. They come ready-made or can be made in a variety of gauges and sizes.

jump ring

soldered ring

split ring

Soldered rings are closed rings that can be used with crimped flexible beading wire, wire-wrapped pieces, or bead tips. Soldered rings are the most secure ring choice.

Split rings are formed like small key rings. They are used to securely attach clasps and charms to a chain or other rings. **Split ring pliers** (see page 43) may be used for easy attachment.

CHAPTER FOUR

TOOL BASICS

Having a variety of pliers, cutters, and wireworking tools is essential for any jewelry maker's toolbox. Good tools, proper technique, and lots of practice help produce professional results. Each tool has a specific purpose. The three basic tools — round nose pliers, chain nose pliers, and side cutters — can be supplemented with other wireworking, metalworking, and shaping tools. In addition, a measuring tape, caliper, and a variety of storage containers are extremely useful.

PLIERS AND CUTTERS

Pliers and cutters designed for wireworking are manufactured in several qualities from beginner tools, usually made in Pakistan, to intermediate tools made in Germany, to advanced tools made in Spain or the United States. The quality of these pliers and cutters varies by the type of metal they are made from to the way the tool is crafted. Spring-loaded models of tools are easier to manipulate.

Chain nose pliers are beading pliers with a tapered jaw that is rounded on the outside and flat and smooth on the inside. This wireworking tool is commonly used for crimping and gripping wire.

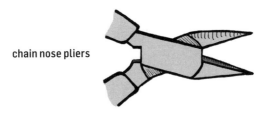

chain nose pliers

Coiling pliers are useful for quickly and easily making uniformly shaped rings, clasps, ear wires, or other findings. These pliers come with jaws of differing diameters from as small as 2 to 5 millimeters to as large as 13 to 20 millimeters.

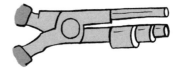

coiling pliers

Crimping pliers are used for crimping tube-shaped crimp beads into neat, folded, flat crimps. This tool is absolutely essential!

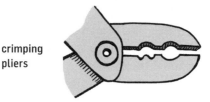

crimping
pliers

Magical crimping pliers are specialty pliers used to transform 2x2 tube crimps into small round beads.

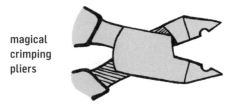

magical
crimping
pliers

Flat nose pliers are beading pliers with a tapered jaw that is smooth and flat on both sides. This tool is useful for projects that require a larger gripping surface or for making chain maille.

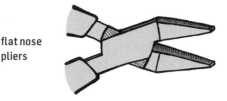

flat nose
pliers

Round nose pliers are beading pliers with smooth, conical barrels that are ideal for making loops. This beading tool is essential for making earrings or any wirework projects that have loops or curves. They are also useful for opening and closing bead tips. Round nose pliers should not be used for gripping.

Split ring pliers are specialty pliers with a small "tooth" on one jaw that will hold open a split ring so that a charm or another ring can be fed onto an existing ring. This tool is especially useful for projects that employ lots of split rings, like charm bracelets.

Flexible beading wire cutters are flush cutters that easily snip through the nylon and metal layers of flexible beading wire. These cutters have small tips for precise cutting of delicate wires.

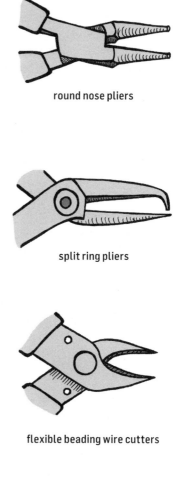

round nose pliers

split ring pliers

flexible beading wire cutters

Memory wire cutters are heavy-duty cutters designed specifically for cutting hard steel memory wire. This specialty tool should always be used to cut memory wire. The blades of other cutting tools are easily damaged when attempting to cut memory wire.

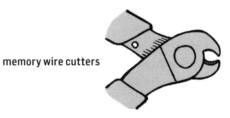

memory wire cutters

Side cutter, sometimes called a **flush cutter,** is an essential beading tool. A side cutter is used to cut hard wire. The blades of a side cutter have a notched side and a flat side that allow for a close cut on small projects.

side cutters

WIRE-SHAPING TOOLS

TOOLS FOR SHAPING WIRE ARE remarkably useful. Wire-shaping tools are available to twist, coil, curl, flatten, and texture wire.

A ball-peen hammer is used to flatten and harden wire and wire shapes. The head is rounded on one end and flat on the other and is usually made of heat-forged steel for strength.

A chasing hammer has a forged steel head that is mounted on a wooden handle. One side of the head has a large face for flattening; the other is a ball-peen side for creating a hammered look.

A mallet has a head made of wood or rubber fastened to a wooden handle. Mallets deliver a softer blow than a metal-headed hammer.

ball-peen
hammer

chasing
hammer

mallet

A **bench block** is a flat steel plate that provides the necessary surface for flattening and hardening wire and wire shapes with wireworking hammers.

A **wire jig** is an amazing tool that aids in the shaping of wire into consistent and even coils, curls, and swirls. To create wire shapes, small pegs are inserted in an evenly spaced grid of holes in a metal or acrylic plate. Wire is wrapped around these pegs in interesting patterns. The shapes are then removed from the jig and hammered to flatten and harden the wire.

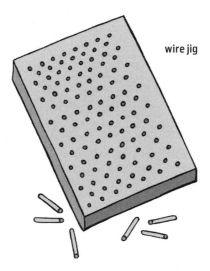

wire jig

MEASURING, POLISHING, AND STORAGE

IN ADDITION TO THE TOOLS mentioned previously, wire-working requires a few other tools that make it easier to complete a full range of projects. While not all of these tools are critical, some techniques are not possible without specific implements.

Measuring Tools

Measuring tools are vitally important. Once beads, findings, and pieces of wire have made their way to storage containers and are no longer labeled with a size, the only way to determine the size is by measuring them individually. Making jewelry also requires knowing a person's ring size, necklace length, or wrist dimension. There are all sorts of measuring tools available to make the job easier.

Calipers are small metal devices with a sliding jaw that makes measuring beads and bead holes very easy. To use a caliper, slide open the jaw, place the bead in the jaw, slide the jaw closed again, and then refer to the measurement guide to determine the size of the bead.

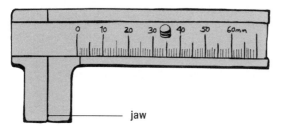

caliper

jaw

A **ring mandrel** is a tapered rod of steel or acrylic used to form, shape, and measure the correct finger size when making a ring. Ring mandrels are usually measured out in quarter ring sizes from 1 to 16.

ring mandrel

A **measuring tape** marked in both inches and centimeters is an important and useful tool to always have on hand. Beads are made and sold in millimeter dimensions, but jewelry is frequently made in inches. Having a tape measure handy makes the conversion so much easier.

A **wire gauge** is a useful tool for easily determining the diameter or thickness of a piece of wire. By running a wire through the various openings, it is possible to figure out the wire's gauge even if the wire is no longer in a marked package.

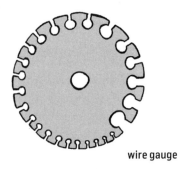
wire gauge

Polishing Products

Polishing products are important for preventing or repairing the effects of tarnishing or oxidization. Most metals will tarnish, oxidize, or darken with time and exposure to air. Metal cleaning and polishing products should always be used with caution and with proper protection for yourself and your surroundings. Regular cleaning and polishing as well as proper storage are the best ways to keep metal jewelry looking its best.

Antitarnish paper is a wonderful product for preventing metal jewelry from tarnishing or oxidizing while pieces are being stored. Add little pieces of antitarnish paper to the bottom of storage containers for the best results.

Jeweler's rouge is a cloth impregnated with a professional compound that cleans and removes tarnish from gold, silver, and other metals. A polishing cloth is then used to buff the metal to a high sheen.

Polishing cloths are easy-to-use, chemically impregnated fabric sheets that remove tarnish or oxidization and polish silver, gold, brass, and copper to their original luster.

Silver dip is a liquid, chemical tarnish remover. Dip or wipe silver to remove tarnish, wash the metal with soap and water, and polish it dry for the best results.

Storage Containers

Storage containers for beads, findings, and tools are not only useful but they protect the materials, keep tools clean and sharp, and keep everything organized. A wide range of containers from screw-top stacking jars to flat, compartmentalized boxes are available. Metals are best stored away from light and in airtight containers.

CHAPTER FIVE

WIREWORK TECHNIQUES

All wirework jewelry grows from the mastery of the basic techniques in this chapter. Learning the basics will allow you to make your own earrings almost immediately. With practice, you'll use these techniques to make links and drops, and to embellish basic wirework jewelry. Mastering these skills and learning some basic metalworking techniques will enable you to make your own clasps and components, and to create intricate wire designs. Take time to learn the basics by practicing with copper or other base metal wires.

SIMPLE LOOP

Making simple loops is a fundamental wirework technique. This method is the most basic skill for making earrings and connecting pieces of wire together.

To make a simple stacked dangle or a basic earring, begin by selecting a head pin in the length that best accommodates the beads and a wire gauge that best matches the bead hole sizes.

1. Stack the bead(s) on a head pin.

2. Use chain nose pliers to bend the head pin against the top bead at a right angle.

3. Use wire cutters to snip the head pin down to ¼ to ½ inch, depending on how large you want the loop.

Tech Tip
If the hole in the bottom bead of the design is too large to stay on the head pin, add a spacer bead or small round bead to the head pin before adding the rest of the beads.

4. Grasp the very tip of the head pin with the round nose pliers (A).

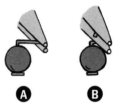

Roll the wire into a circle by rotating the pliers (B).

A   **B**

5. To complete the loop, readjust the tool's grip on the wire. Make sure to grasp the wire at the same point with the barrel of the pliers.

6. Now the loop is complete.

Tech Tip

To open the simple loop for attaching an ear wire or chain, do not unroll the loop. Grasp the open side of the loop with chain nose pliers and bend it away from the base wire. To close the loop, simply reverse this action by bringing the end of the loop back to the base wire. This will prevent misshaping the loop.

WIRE-WRAPPED LOOP

Wire-wrapped loops are more secure than simple loops. Mastering this technique can take practice, but it is an essential wireworking technique. Wire-wrapped loops can be used for making earrings or for connecting pieces of wire and beads.

When making a basic earring or simple stacked dangle, begin by selecting a head pin in the length that best accommodates the beads. Next choose the wire gauge that best matches the bead hole sizes.

1. Use chain nose pliers to grasp the wire above the stacked beads.

2. Leave a small gap above the top bead and use the same pliers to bend the wire at a 90-degree angle.

3. Switch to round nose pliers. Hold them so the barrels are vertical, and grasp the wire at the bend. Bend the wire up and over the top barrel of the pliers to form half of the loop. The top barrel of the pliers is now inside the loop.

4. Remove the pliers and move the half loop onto the bottom barrel of the tool. Keep bending the wire around the bottom barrel of the tool to complete the loop. Then let go of the loop.

5. Hold the loop flat with chain nose pliers. Do not insert the jaw back into the loop.

6. Use your fingers to wrap the wire tail tightly around the base wire, creating neat stacks. Make sure to start just below the loop and wrap downward toward the beads.

7. Use wire cutters to clip the excess wire carefully, and use chain nose pliers to push the clipped end into the coil.

Tech Tip

If you are attaching a chain or another loop, slip it on at step 4, before you complete the loops.

WIRE-WRAPPED BEAD CAP

Wire-wrapped bead caps are a simple way to add a finished look to bead dangles or pendants. To make a simple pendant, begin by selecting a head pin or piece of wire in the length that best accommodates the beads. Next choose the wire gauge that best matches the bead hole sizes. Complete steps 1 through 4 of the wire-wrapped loop technique (see page 53), and then continue with the following steps.

1. Grasp the loop from the side with chain nose pliers. Do not insert the jaw back into the loop.

2. Wrap the wire tail tightly around the base wire one full revolution.

3. Continue to wrap down to the top of the bead in tight, concentric coils. Wrap so the coil lies neatly against the bead.

4. Use wire cutters to clip the excess wire carefully.

WIRE-WRAPPED LINK WITH BEADS

Wire-wrapped links with beads can be used as elements in a jewelry design or linked together to make a chain. Individual links are added into a design as they are being made.

1. Cut a piece of wire approximately 4 inches longer than the bead. Begin by grasping the wire 1½ inches from one end with chain nose pliers. Bend the wire at a right angle.

2. Holding round nose pliers so the barrels are vertical, grasp the wire at the bend. Use your fingers to bend the wire up and over the top barrel of the pliers to form half of the loop. The top barrel of the pliers is now inside the loop.

3. Remove the pliers and move the half loop onto the bottom barrel of the tool. Keep bending the wire around the bottom barrel of the tool to complete the loop. Then let go of the loop.

4. Hold the loop flat using chain nose pliers. Do not insert the jaw back into the loop.

5. Wrap the wire tail tightly around the base wire. Wrap so the coil creates neat stacks. Make sure to start just below the loop and wrap downward.

6. Once you have finished wrapping, use wire cutters to carefully clip the excess wire close to the last coil of the wrap; then use flat nose pliers to push this clipped end into the wrap.

7. Turn the wire upright and string the bead onto the tail.

8. Create a second wire-wrapped loop of the wire, again pushing the clipped end into the wrap. The link is now complete.

WIRE-WRAPPED LINK CHAIN

To make a wire-wrapped link chain, begin by making your first link using the wire-wrapped link technique (see page 56). Start your second link by completing steps 1 through 3 of the wire-wrapped link technique, then proceed with the directions below.

Slip the unwrapped loop into a finished loop of your completed link.

Return to steps 4 through 8 of the wire-wrapped link technique to create a second finished link. Continue by making and adding additional links until the desired length of wire-wrapped link chain is complete.

BRIOLETTE WRAP

The briolette wrap technique may be used with any top-drilled bead or briolette to create a drop, charm, or pendant. It can also be used to create a bail to suspend a donut-shaped bead. A bail (sometimes spelled *bale*) is a jewelry-making component designed to attach a pendant or stone to a necklace. Bails are either ready-made metal components that are glued to a pendant or stone, or handcrafted wire components that are wrapped onto a pendant or stone. In all cases, the chain or stringing material passes through the loop at the top of the bail so that the pendant or stone can hang from the necklace, usually in the center front.

The briolette wrap is an important wireworking skill to master. To make a simple briolette drop, begin by selecting a wire in the gauge that best matches the bead hole.

1. Cut a piece of wire approximately 4 inches longer than the width of the briolette drill hole. With teardrop briolettes, the width of the drill hole is quite short, but with flat, pear-shaped briolettes, the width of the drill hole will be longer. When you are first learning to make briolette wraps, a longer piece of wire is easier to work with.

 String the briolette onto the wire so that one side of the wire is shorter and one side is longer as shown. Bend both sides of the wire up along the tip of the briolette. Cross one side of the wire over the other, across the tip of the briolette.

2. Use chain nose pliers to bend the longer, front-facing wire about 45 degrees, so that it points straight up from the tip of the briolette. This wire is now the base wire.

longer end

shorter end

3. Begin to wrap the shorter, rear-facing wire around the base wire.

4. Continue to wrap this wire around the base wire one full rotation.

5. Use wire cutters to clip off the remainder of the wrapping wire.

6. Make a wire-wrapped loop (see page 53) with the remaining base wire.

COVERING A BRIOLETTE

For a more decorative look or for making briolette pendants, try covering the top of a briolette with wire. Complete steps 1 through 4 of the briolette wrap technique (see page 59). When covering a briolette with wire, you will need to start with a longer piece of wire. The length of your wire depends on the size of the briolette and how many wraps you will be making.

1. Instead of cutting the excess wire in step 5 of the briolette wrap technique, continue to wrap the wire around the base wire and down to the top of the briolette in concentric coils.

2. For a neatly wrapped bead cap, make sure each coil of wire lies neatly against the wire from the previous row.

3. Use wire cutters to clip the excess wrapped wire. Gently tuck the end of the wire into the last wrap with chain nose pliers.

MAKING BASIC EAR WIRES

Making ear wires is a wonderful way to make personalized earrings.

1. Begin by cutting a 3-inch piece of wire. Make a simple loop (see page 51).

2. Holding the loop with chain nose pliers, use your fingers to bend the wire up and over the small end of a ring mandrel to create the ear wire.

3. With the chain nose pliers, grip the end of the wire and bend it up slightly.

4. Cut the end of the wire and file it smooth. Repeat to make the second ear wire.

Tech Tip

To make identically sized ear wires, mark the ring mandrel with a piece of tape. This will ensure that the wire is bent in the same place for both ear wires.

MAKING HEAD PINS AND EYE PINS

Head pins and eye pins are essential jewelry-making components used for stacking and dangling beads. The "head" or the "eye" of the pin prevents the beads from falling off the end of the wire. Head pins and eye pins are often used to make simple earrings or to dangle beads from a chain.

Head pins and eye pins can be purchased ready-made, or you can make your own. Begin by selecting a gauge that works with the size of the beads and a wire material that works with the other metals being used in the project.

BASIC HEAD PIN

To make a basic head pin, cut a length of wire and use flat nose pliers to make a tiny bend at the tip of the wire. Pinch this bend tightly against the base wire of the head pin.

PADDLE-STYLE HEAD PIN

To make a paddle-style head pin, use a mallet and a bench block to hammer the end of the wire instead of bending it. The flattened, widened tip will prevent beads from falling off the end of the wire.

SPIRAL-STYLE HEAD PIN

To make a spiral-style head pin, start by making a basic head pin. Grip the bent tip of the wire with chain nose pliers and coil the base wire. The size of the spiral will depend on design, the size of the bead holes, or how decorative you want the head pin to be.

BASIC EYE PIN

To make a basic eye pin, cut a length of wire and use round nose pliers to make a simple loop (see page 51) at the tip of the wire.

MAKING HOOP EARRINGS

Beading hoops are a common jewelry-making component used primarily for making hoop earrings. They are also used for making wine stem charms. Beading hoops can be purchased ready-made, or they can be made in a variety of metals, sizes, and gauges.

BASIC 2-INCH BEADING HOOPS

1. Decide on the diameter of your finished beading hoop. (The diameter is the measurement across the width of the hoop at its fullest point.) Cut a length of wire four times this measurement. For example a 2-inch hoop will require 8 inches of wire. Wrap the wire one complete revolution around a mandrel, spool, or other cylindrical object that is the same diameter as the desired finished hoop.

2. Remove the wire from the mandrel. Prepare to make the closure by cutting the ends of the wire so they overlap by ¼ inch.

3. Make a simple loop (see page 51) at one end of the wire.

4. Use chain nose pliers to bend ¼ inch of the free end of the hoop at a 90-degree angle. (If using ready-made hoops, start here.)

5. To close the hoop, hook the bent end of the hoop into the loop end.

....

Embellishing Hoop Earrings

After purchasing or making basic hoops (see facing page), embellish them with beads or charms for added interest.

String beads, charms, or dangles onto the free end of the hoop before bending the end to make the hook.

String small beads or rondelles on fine gauge wire and carefully position and wrap the small beads around the wire of the hoop.

....

WORKING WITH CONES

This technique is essential for completing multistrand necklaces with a finished look that hides knots, crimp beads, or bead tips.

1. Cut 3 inches of wire and make a wire-wrapped loop (see page 53). The size of this loop depends on the number of strands that will be attached and the size of the cone. For a two- or three-strand project, a small loop is sufficient. For four or more strands, a larger loop is preferable.

2. Individually crimp each strand of beads to the loop. Use one crimp per strand.

3. String the cone onto the wire and over the wire-wrapped loop and crimped bead strands.

4. String a small bead onto the wire and start another wire wrap. String one side of the clasp onto the loop and finish the wire wrap. Repeat on the other end with the remaining side of the clasp.

Tech Tip

If you are using nylon or silk, use bead tips instead of crimps to attach the strands to the loop.

FINISHING MEMORY WIRE

Memory wire is a unique type of wire, perfect for making necklaces, bracelets, anklets, and rings. The wire is spring-tempered steel, so it always springs back to its original coil form. Memory wire comes raw or as plated silver, gold, or brass steel.

Because memory wire is made from steel, it can be hard to manipulate. Using good tools and proper technique makes memory wire easier to work with. Two methods are used to finish memory wire.

METHOD #1

1. Dab a drop of super glue on one end of the memory wire and insert it into a half-drilled memory wire end cap.

2. String the beads and glue a second memory wire end cap to the other end of the memory wire.

METHOD #2

1. Use round nose pliers to roll the very end of the memory wire into a loop. (Refer to the simple loop technique on page 51.)

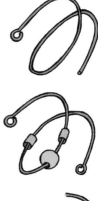

2. String the beads and finish the other end of the memory wire by making a second loop.

3. Embellish the loop ends of the memory wire jewelry by adding a dangle or charm.

Tech Tip

Begin any project by cutting the desired number of coils of memory wire using memory wire cutters. Using regular wire cutters or nippers on memory wire can damage the blades. Always use cutters specially designed for cutting memory wire.

HOW TO OPEN AND CLOSE JUMP RINGS

Many pieces of strung jewelry use jump rings to connect the clasp or to add charms or pendants. It is important to properly open and close jump rings when adding a clasp or charm. This ensures the long-term integrity of the jump ring.

1. Grasp the jump ring from one side with flat nose pliers.

2. Using your fingers or another pair of flat nose pliers, push one side of the loop away from the other.

3. Do not pull the loop apart, as this motion will eventually break the wire. Your open jump ring should look like this from the side.

4. Slip on a chain, charm, or finding. Use the same method to close the jump ring. Wiggle the ends of the ring or loop back and forth to close any gap.

HOW TO USE SPLIT RING PLIERS

Split ring pliers are a very specialized tool used exclusively to open split rings without stretching them out or damaging them. A split ring is a continuous double circle of wire coiled like a key ring. Split rings are sturdier than jump rings and are not likely to open accidentally. The split ring plier is a very handy tool for opening and holding split rings open.

split ring pliers

1. Place the tip of the curved part of the jaw of the split ring pliers between the layers of the coil, near one of the ends. Squeeze down on the tool to open the coil.

2. While holding the split ring open, slip a chain, charm, or clasp onto the end of the coil.

3. Remove the split ring pliers. Slide the chain, charm, or clasp around the coil until it moves freely around both coils of the split ring.

HOW TO USE WIRE CUTTERS

Wire cutters are used to cut hard wire and flexible beading wire and are one of the three basic tools that should be in every jewelry maker's toolbox. Wire cutters designed specifically for jewelry making are superior to the tools available at the hardware store. Their blades are smaller and angled to make small, flush cuts on small-gauge wires.

1. Look at both sides of your wire cutters. Notice that one side is flush (flat) and the other is slightly recessed.

2. Always place the flush side of your wire cutters as close as possible to the part of the wire that will be left on your piece.

3. This technique gives the closest cut and leaves the least amount of leftover wire.

Tech Tip

It is a good idea to have separate wire cutters for hard wire and flexible beading wire. Using hard wire cutters exclusively for cutting hard wire will keep the blades of the flexible beading wire cutters sharper longer.

GLOSSARY

Alloy. An alloy is made by combining metal elements to improve the strength, durability, color, or melting point of a single metal element. It can be a less valuable base metal combination, such as brass or bronze, or a more valuable precious metal combination, such as sterling silver and karat gold.

Annealing. A multistep process of heating and stressing metal to improve its strength and hardness.

Anodization. An electrochemical process that permanently alters the surface of nonferrous metals, making them corrosion resistant. Aluminum is frequently anodized.

Base metal. Base metals — copper, iron, and nickel — corrode or oxidize easily. Base metal is also a generic term used to describe all metals and alloys that are not otherwise classified as precious metals.

Corrosion. The process of deterioration that occurs when certain metals are exposed to water or oxygen.

Draw plate. A hardened, steel plate pierced with a number of holes in decreasing sizes. Wire is pulled through successively smaller holes on the draw plate to make it thinner.

Ductility. The physical quality of a metal that allows it to be drawn or stretched without cracking or breaking.

Fusing. To mix metals together by melting.

Gauge. Gauge is a numerical representation of the diameter of round wire or the cross-sectional dimension of shaped wire.

Hypoallergenic. Metals that tend to cause fewer allergic skin reactions than other metals.

Karat. A numerical representation of the percentage of pure gold found in a gold alloy. Karat is not to be confused with *carat*, a term that refers to the weight of diamonds and other precious gemstones.

Luster. The way light reflects off the surface of metal, causing it to glow.

Malleability. The physical quality of a metal that allows it to be manipulated, compressed, hammered, and rolled.

Ounce. A measurement of weight most commonly used in the United States. There are 16 ounces in 1 pound.

Pennyweight. A unit of measure equal to $\frac{1}{20}$ troy ounce. In the Middle Ages, money was based on the weight of sterling silver. A British penny was $\frac{1}{20}$ ounce or $\frac{1}{240}$ pound of sterling silver.

Plating or electroplating. The process of applying a thin layer of precious metal or alloy to the surface of a conductive material, namely another metal, with electricity.

Tarnish. A thin layer of corrosion that forms over certain metals when they are exposed to air, causing the metal to darken and lose its luster.

Temper. The hardness or softness of a particular wire. Tempers range from dead-soft to spring-hard.

Troy ounce. An imperial measurement of weight. There are about 32 troy ounces in 1 kilogram.

APPENDIX

Types of Metal

The type of metal chosen for a jewelry project is largely a matter of personal preference. Things to consider when selecting a metal are cost, workability, and, of course, color. Precious metals are the most sought after, but they are also the most costly. Metal alloys and precious metal-plated base metals are attractive and cost-effective alternatives.

By definition, the terms *precious* and *base* are chemical references that describe the corrosive qualities of different metals. In the marketplace, these terms are used to categorize metals by their rarity and their value. The precious metals, also known as *noble metals*, that are desirable for jewelry making include gold, silver, and platinum. These metals are highly resistant to corrosion, though silver will tarnish. Precious metals are easier to work with because they are more malleable and they have a naturally shinier luster than other metals. Precious metals are also commodities, and their cost fluctuates daily with the world markets.

Base metal elements, including iron, nickel, and copper, occur naturally in large quantities. The abundance of these elements makes wire and metal components made from base metal alloys far less expensive than precious metals. *Base metal* is also a generic term used to describe all metals used in jewelry making that are not classified as precious metals. Base metal alloys include pewter, brass, and bronze.

GOLD

Gold (Au) has been popular for its rarity and beauty since before written history. Gold is the most malleable of all metals, making it the easiest to work with. Because pure gold is generally too soft to work with when making wire, chain, and jewelry findings, it is mixed with other metals, including copper and zinc, to produce karat gold. The term *karat* refers to the percentage of pure gold in popular karat weights, which ranges from 10K to 24k (see table on page 80).

Gold-filled (G/F) is a process by which 14K or 18K gold is bonded to a base metal, usually brass but sometimes copper. Generally 5% of the total weight and the entire surface of a gold-filled item is karat gold.

Gold-plate (G/P) is a process by which a thin layer of karat gold is electroplated to a base metal like brass or steel. The gold-plated layer is thinner than the layer applied in gold-filled wire and will wear off over time.

Vermeil [ver-mey] is a process by which 24K or 18K, but no less than 14K gold, is flash-plated or micron-plated to a sterling silver or fine silver core. Flash-plating involves dipping or washing a silver core in electroplating solution for a very short period of time. The gold surface of flash-plated vermeil can wear off in a matter of days. Micron-plating involves soaking a silver core in electroplating solution for an extended period of time until a 1 to 2.5 micron layer of gold has coated the surface. The gold surface of micron-plated vermeil will also wear off in time.

White gold is an alloy of gold and white metals like zinc, nickel, or silver. Even though white gold is tarnish resistant, it is brittle and usually needs to be rhodium-plated. White gold is a cost-effective alternative to platinum but can cause allergic reactions once the plating wears off.

Rose gold is an alloy of gold and copper that results in a golden metal with a reddish or pinkish hue. Typically, the ratio of gold to copper is 3 to 1, but other percentages can be found. The lightness or darkness of the rose hue results from the amount of copper added. Rose gold will patina over time.

Rose gold–filled is a process that permanently bonds a layer of rose gold alloy to a base metal alloy like copper, nickel, or brass.

Karat (K) Gold

KARAT (K)	PURE GOLD CONTENT	USE IN JEWELRY
24	100% (pure gold)	Too soft for most jewelry; very popular in some parts of the world
22	.917 (91.7%)	Too soft for some jewelry; very popular in some parts of the world
18	.75 (75%)	Good choice for jewelry; excellent balance of strength and value
14	.585 (58.5%)	Very popular for jewelry; good balance of durability and value
10	.417 (41.7%)	Lowest gold content allowed to be marketed as gold in the United States

SILVER

Silver (Ag) is a very soft, easily formed, silvery white metal. Oxidation will cause silver to darken or tarnish over time.

Silver is frequently mixed with other metals to make it more durable for use in jewelry-making components.

Fine silver has a .999 level of purity. Fine silver is the purest and softest silver available. Thai silver beads and findings, which are often elaborately stamped, are made from fine silver.

Sterling silver has a .925 level of purity. This silver alloy is made from 92.5% pure silver and 7.5% copper. True sterling silver will always be stamped ".925."

Argentium is a modern sterling silver alloy that contains 92.5% pure silver and 7.5% copper and germanium. Germanium gives this alloy increased tarnish resistance and prevents fire scale. These properties make Argentium a very desirable, though expensive, metal.

Silver-filled is a process by which fine silver or sterling silver is bonded to a base metal alloy like nickel or brass. The total weight of a silver-filled item is notated as either $\frac{1}{10}$ (5%) or $\frac{1}{20}$ (10%) fine silver or sterling silver.

Silver-plate is a process by which a thin layer of fine silver or sterling silver is electroplated to a base metal like brass or steel. The silver-plated layer is thinner than the silver-filled layer and will wear off over time.

OTHER METALS

Nickel (Ni) looks like silver but can cause a skin reaction in many people. It is a tough, corrosion-resistant material that is easily molded and often used as an element is metal alloys.

Nickel silver (also known as German silver or gun metal) is not silver at all. It is a silvery, hard, corrosion-resistant, malleable alloy of 65% copper, 18% zinc, and 17% nickel.

Stainless steel is a metal alloy that contains 90% steel and 10% chromium. Since it does not corrode, rust, or tarnish, it is an attractive metal for jewelry-making components.

Surgical steel (SSS) is a medical-grade, corrosion-resistant, and rust-resistant stainless steel that is hypoallergenic.

Pewter is a malleable, silver-toned alloy containing 90% tin and 10% copper. The addition of copper is used to harden the alloy. Low-quality pewter, with a bluish tint, is hardened with lead, which is considered to be carcinogenic. Pewter has a very low melting point that makes it ideal for casting.

Britannia is a pewter alloy containing 92% tin, 6% antimony, and 2% copper. It is essentially lead and cadmium free.

Copper (Cu) is the oldest-known metal and is often associated with having healing powers. It is a reddish-brown, metallic element that patinas to a warm brown. Copper can also take on a green patina with oxidization. Copper is often an element in metal alloys.

Bronze (Bz) is an alloy of 90% copper and 10% tin.

Brass (Br) is an alloy of 75% copper and 25% zinc that is gold in color. Brass will tarnish and turn brown over time.

Niobium (Nb) is a soft gray metal with very low toxicity, which makes it hypoallergenic.

INDEX

Page numbers in *italic* indicate illustrations; page numbers in **bold** indicate charts.